# Positive Affirmations

## Daily affirmations for attracting health, healing, and happiness into your life.

A FeelFabToday Guide
By Rachel Robins

Positive Affirmations

Copyright © 2014 Rachel Robins

Cover and internal vector images credited to:
© wenani © variant © julydfg / depositphotos

ISBN-13: 978-1500459956
ISBN-10: 150045995X

# Table of Contents

# 1

## How This Book Can Help You Attract Health, Healing, And Happiness

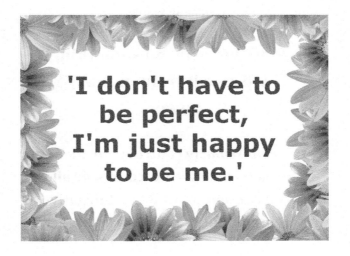

'I don't have to be perfect, I'm just happy to be me.'

*"It's the repetition of affirmations that leads to belief. And once that belief becomes a deep conviction, things begin to happen."*
*~ Muhammad Ali*

Muhammad Ali unquestioningly understood the power of affirmations. When he proclaimed, *'I am the greatest'* as the little known boxer, Cassius Clay, he was setting the wheels in motion for his momentous achievements in the world of boxing.

Positive affirmations can be used to transform our lives in some exceptional ways. They can permanently alter the way we think, reprogram our mind to move away from damaging self-beliefs, and allow us to pursue and achieve the life we really want.

## When we focus on something, we give it tremendous power.

**Do you *consciously* control your thoughts to focus on positive outcomes, or allow your *subconscious* mind to let negative or unhelpful thoughts prevail?**

Throughout this book, we'll explore **what** positive affirmations are all about, **why** they are so powerful at affecting change, and **how** to integrate them effortlessly into your daily life.

**Inside this book you'll discover:**

- **What** affirmations really are
- **Why** they are so powerful

- **How** to use them productively
- **Simple** techniques to radically alter your subconscious thoughts
- **Actionable** steps to replace negative thoughts
- **Empowering** tips to ensure your personal affirmation statements really work
- **Positive** affirmation examples

Because the power of affirmations lies within the subconscious mind, we'll look at various techniques you can use to influence your thoughts, attract good things into your life, and deliver the successful outcomes you desire.

> # Positive affirmations
> # help illuminate the
> # very things you
> # seek to attract

We focus on ways in which you can improve your health, heal your body and mind, and move toward daily happiness, through the consistent use of positive affirmations.

We'll help you discover the specific areas in your life that are most important for influencing change, and identify ways to create your own personal positive belief statements.

When you remove mental barriers, replace negative self-talk, and develop empowering affirmation habits, you'll reap the benefits immediately. Our aim is to provide you with ideas, inspiration, and encouragement to craft your own uplifting affirmation statements, which will repeatedly deliver the rewards you desire.

When you apply the techniques in this book, and are consistent with your actions, you'll have taken a massive step toward creating your ideal future.

**You'll be empowered to:**

- **Stop** negative thoughts or self-doubt holding you back
- **Start** focusing on positive change
- **Control** your subconscious thoughts with uplifting affirmations
- **Feel** happier, healthier, and healed

As you develop new skills and positive affirmation habits, your overall health and happiness should improve, leaving you feeling energized and empowered.

We hope you'll find inspiration and guidance so you can immediately benefit from your new, personally designed, daily affirmation statements.

## 2

# What Are Positive Affirmations?

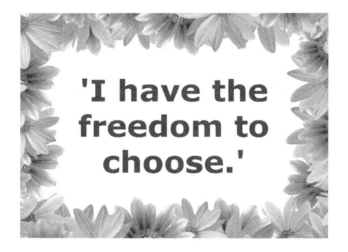

*"Affirmations are our mental vitamins,*
*providing the supplementary positive thoughts*
*we need to balance the barrage of negative events*
*and thoughts we experience daily."*
*~ Tia Walker*

## *So, What Are Positive Affirmations?*

Affirmations are short, positive, powerful statements, which you can repeat to yourself as often as required. They are a highly effective tool, which can be used to create positive and lasting change in your life.

Put simply, they are positive phrases about yourself, which describe how or what you would like to be, or would like to attract into your life.

### *Affirmations definition - dictionary.com*
-   the act or an instance of affirmations; state of being affirmed.
-   the assertion that something exists or is true.
-   something that is affirmed; a statement or proposition that is declared to be true.
-   confirmation or ratification of the truth or validity of a prior judgment, decision, etc.
-   Law. a solemn declaration accepted instead of a statement under oath.

A positive affirmation in itself is a beneficial thought or belief that you focus on specifically to produce, or increase, a desired result. Affirmations can be an effective method of self-improvement, enabling you to boost your confidence, reduce negativity, improve self-belief, and affect positive change in many areas of your life.

**For example, you could focus on the following:**

- Health – *'I feel fitter and more energized every day.'*
- Healing – *'Today I will make resting and healing my main priority.'*
- Happiness – *'I don't have to be perfect, I'm just happy to be me.'*

Unfortunately, affirmations can also be negative, taking the form of negative self-talk, self-limiting beliefs, and low levels of confidence or self-esteem. The purpose of positive affirmations is to affect change in the way we think about ourselves, about others, and the world in general. When used correctly and consistently, they can help drive positive, permanent change in our thought processes. Additionally, they can manage our expectations for positive results, and, in turn, our ability to experience the outcomes we desire.

The process of learning and practicing positive affirmations can lead to the rewiring of our subconscious mind. Consequently we can reverse the effects of negative habits or beliefs, and replace them with new set of positive behaviors and self-nurturing beliefs. Plus, our goals become clearer and more achievable, and our level of self-belief will improve immeasurably.

A well-crafted personal statement, which positively resonates at an emotional level, can be a powerful tool to change your perspective on life. However, the *way* we structure our personal phrases is extremely important. For an affirmation to be effective, it must be positive, set in the present tense, centered only on things you do want, and not what you don't.

**Affirmations can take the form of:**

- Verbal statements
- Silent repeated thoughts
- Written statements
- Audio recordings

Although positive affirmations can produce some amazing results, many people initially find them difficult to grasp. They can feel strange, seem unbelievable, and appear to be ineffective. There are many reasons as to why affirmations don't work, which we will discuss later in the book. The good news is there are specific solutions that enable us to overcome these issues, *and* to boost their effectiveness.

The mindful application of positive affirmations can help to reduce, or eliminate, the effect of negative thinking. It can also be a powerful method for building strength in areas of our lives we most desire, for healing areas of weakness, and for allowing us to create the optimal future we aspire to.

## *Types of Affirmations*

There are various different types of affirmations, some being more appropriate than others, depending on your requirements.

Affirmations can be kept simple, can be extended slightly, or can be made longer and more descriptive. **For example:**

- *'I am healthy.'*
- *'I love my body and am grateful to be in full health.'*
- *'I love my body and am grateful to be in full health. I honor my body by eating nutritious foods, getting plenty of exercise, and spending time on rest and relaxation, every day. I make well-being and health a top priority.'*

Shorter affirmations are easier to remember, and to repeat quickly and often. The longer ones allow you to define a wider range of target areas, and to encompass these into your daily focus.

There are affirmation statements you can make for different areas of your life. Depending on which areas you seek improvement in, or which parts of your life you would most like to influence, you can choose to focus on *categories* such as:

- Health/wellness
- Healing/self-care
- Stress/anxiety
- Self-confidence/self-esteem
- Happiness
- Managing fears/doubts
- Forgiveness/letting go/peace
- Love/relationships
- Friendship
- Personal growth/knowledge
- Money/abundance
- Career/business
- Religion/spirituality
- Creativity/fun

There are also different *styles* of affirmations you can choose, depending on the type of influence you want to assert:

**Acceptance Affirmations**
An acceptance style of affirmations enables you to be open to receiving good things into your life. They focus

on the gaining of benefit, and the acceptance of the good things you currently have, and will continue to have in the future.

- *'I accept (myself for who I am).'*
- *'I am open (to new experiences and opportunities).'*
- *'I allow (my body to heal and get better each day).'*
- *'Every day, I gain (more confidence).'*
- *'I acquire (more helpful knowledge each day I study).'*

## Action Oriented Affirmations

An action oriented affirmation is a statement you make about an action or step you are focusing on. They allow you to move forward with authority, and to be decisive in your actions.

- *'I move forward (with my healing and pain reduction).'*
- *'I make (decisions based on my well-being and the well-being of others).'*
- *'Each step I take (today makes a positive difference tomorrow).'*
- *'I act (with full knowledge and specific intent).'*
- *'I walk (tall and with confidence).'*

## Letting Go Affirmations

An affirmation that focuses on letting go is an opportunity to release negative influences, unlock areas that hold you back and re-write destructive self-beliefs. They can be cleansing, allowing you to purge negative thoughts and let go of unwanted emotional baggage.

- *'I release (the anger toward the person who caused my accident).'*
- *'I let go of (negative memories and focus on a positive future).'*
- *'I permit myself to (be happy).'*
- *'I am free to (walk away from toxic relationships).'*
- *'I forgive (myself for past mistakes).'*

## Intention Affirmations

Clearly stating your intentions can be a powerful way to create change. Linking your intent to a specific purpose can help to determine a positive result in the areas of your life you care about the most.

- *'I intend to (overcome my fear of dentists and seek the help I need).'*
- *'My mission is (to eat 3 healthy, balanced meals per day).'*
- *'I build (new levels of confidence every day).'*

- *'I resolve (to live my life to the fullest).'*
- *'My intention today (is to be calm, relaxed and happy).'*

## Incorporating Affirmations

The aim of these affirmations is to combine and integrate your thoughts deep into your subconscious, so they become a natural part of your being.

- *'I combine (all my new knowledge on healthy eating into my daily routines).'*
- *'I integrate (positivity into every action I take).'*
- *'I incorporate (love into my daily actions).'*
- *'Today (will be a happy day).'*
- *'I blend (energy and enthusiasm into everything I do).'*

## Gratitude Affirmations

These allow you to give thanks for the good in your life.

- *'I am grateful (for my health and happiness).'*
- *'I am thankful (for those who love and care for me).'*
- *'I thank (God for all that has been given to me).'*
- *'I am gratified by (the kindness of others).'*

- *'I am content (with my life as it is).'*

As you can see, there are different types of affirmations, which you can select, according to your needs. You may choose ones that suit your purpose at a given time, or you may find it relevant to move through the various stages. For example, if you are on a journey:

**Letting Go -** *'I let go of (negative memories and focus on a positive future).'*

**Acceptance -** *'I accept (myself for who I am).'*

**Action Oriented -** *'I walk (tall and with confidence).'*

**Intention -** *'I build (new levels of confidence every day).'*

**Incorporating -** *'I integrate (positivity into every action I take).'*

**Gratitude -** *'I am thankful (for those who love and care for me).'*

There is no right or wrong, in terms of selecting the type of affirmations to use. However, to be effective, they do need to be relevant to your desired outcome, and to really resonate with you at an emotional level.

## *Reflections of Your Purpose and Value*

Affirmations can be a powerful method for pursuing and developing the things you desire, in a purposeful manner. When you have a specific goal in mind, or a desire to achieve something that has a strong meaning to you, you need to use tools and methods that will provide you with your desired result.

When you spend time, attention or energy on activities that go against your personal values, or lead you away from your goals, you can end up feeling dissatisfied, negative or stressed. Fortunately, affirmations that are aligned with your purpose can help get you back on track, and to take control of your thoughts and actions.

Research (carried out in Psychological Science November 2005 vol. 16 no. 11 846-851) identified that affirmations of personal value can help to reduce the impact of stress, on both an emotional and physical level. They worked with 85 participants, to test their stress response to a laboratory set stress challenge. Some participants were asked to complete a value-affirmation task prior to taking the stress test, and those in control group were not. The ones who carried out the value-affirmation beforehand, showed considerably lower cortisol (a.k.a. the stress hormone) responses to stress, in comparison with those in the control group.

Additionally, participants who had naturally higher levels of self-esteem and optimism, and who carried out the value-affirmation task, produced the lowest level of stress response after the test. The researchers concluded that reflecting on personal values can help to lower the impact of physical and psychological stress responses.

**Check that your affirmations are reflecting *your* personal values and true sense of purpose.**

**Ask yourself the following:**

- What are you passionate about and would love to achieve?
- Do you want to make a difference in the world, or to change something significant?
- Is there something you would like to have more of in life?
- What outcome are you truly looking for?
- What motivates you to take action?
- Do you have a clear sense of purpose, possibly in different areas of your life?
- What are *your* personal values, and what do you cherish?

- Do your affirmations clearly link to your purpose or values?

When you align your affirmations to your personal values and to a true sense of purpose, you have strongly positioned yourself to achieve some fantastic outcomes.

## *Ways To Make Affirmations Work*

Although affirmations can be a highly successful tool to help create significant change, to influence how you feel, and to direct you toward positive outcomes, you need to know *how* to make them work for you. There are many ways to practice and carry out your affirmations; however you must employ effective methods to ensure they produce the results you desire.

If you are trying to alter a set of negative beliefs or self-esteem issues, then firstly you'll need to identify exactly what those specific issues are, to start the healing and creation process. It is also important to create self-affirmation statements that resonate deeply within you, and that your mind does not reject or resist.

Affirmations work by reprogramming the subconscious mind, and altering the way you automatically think about certain subjects. Therefore, an understanding of this process, and your ability to positively affect your subconscious thoughts, is an important step toward successfully implementing positive affirmations.

*"Success will be within your reach only when you start reaching out for it."*
*~ Stephen Richards*

When you begin to challenge negative self-beliefs, and to use positive, supportive statements instead, you'll become more and more aware of the effect your choice of words and thoughts have on your life. In Chapter 4, we take a detailed look at **how** to successfully implement positive affirmations, and to work with them until those positive statements become an automatic part of your belief structure.

## 3

# Why Use Positive Affirmations?

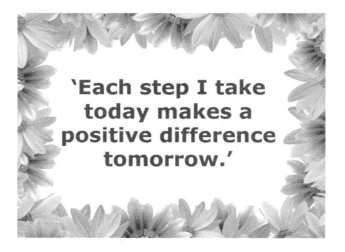

'Each step I take today makes a positive difference tomorrow.'

The power of correctly applied affirmations cannot be underestimated. These powerful statements send triggers to your subconscious to work in harmony with your aspirations. They help you to mentally prepare for your desired outcome, and they bring energy to whatever you focus on.

## *Reasons They Don't Work*

If you've tried to work with affirmations before, yet found they haven't worked for you, then it's tempting to write them off as ineffective. However, there are various reasons why affirmations can fail to work, which, fortunately, do not mean they can't work for you in the future.

### Resistance

We should start this section by recognizing that affirmations need to sit comfortably with you. Any sense your subconscious has that you are not speaking the 'truth', and it will resist or reject the words you're saying. You can't force your subconscious to believe a lie, instead you need to create personal statements that you find believable, and that feel right.

Your subconscious mind is not easily fooled, and will accept a truth, but fight against something that jars against its core beliefs. For example, you might say '*I am a fit, healthy, perfect 170lbs*', when in reality you are over your optimal weight at 200lbs, and can't walk up the stairs without struggling for breath. As you say the words, your mind will be in immediate conflict with that statement, and the internal rejection will not help to embed the statement as a new belief.

If, instead, you make a statement such as '*Today I am moving toward my ideal weight of 170lbs, and am becoming fitter and healthier every day'*, then your mind will be able to support this as a truth (providing you also support your desire with relevant actions).

*"It's the constant and determined effort that breaks down all resistance, sweeps away all obstacles."*
~ *Claude M. Bristol*

## Rejection

If a negative belief you hold is extremely strong, then again, you will have difficulties with your mind permitting you to change the belief. If you try to repeat *'I am beautiful'* when you have deep internal issues with your appearance, or self-esteem, then affirmations of this type will seldom work alone.

Instead, you will need to take the affirmation process slowly and steadily, using statements such as *'I am becoming the person I want to be.'* or *'I am thankful for each day that I allow my inner and outer beauty to shine through.'*

Affirmations can be a powerful part of a journey, when you're aiming to alter previously held negative beliefs, and transform them into positive, self-supporting beliefs. However, deeply held negative beliefs can be hard to re-wire, and excessively strong ones may need to be approached through a combination of techniques, possibly with professional guidance.

## Making Things Worse

As with the resistance and rejection notes above, the incorrect use of positive affirmations can actually make some people feel worse. Statements such as *'I am lovable'*, when the person 'knows' they are not, reinforces their belief that they are not. Statements such as this, for someone suffering from low self-esteem, will prompt their mind to immediately find the counter argument and state *'No, you're not.'* The strengthening of their negative self-belief deepens. The use of affirmations in this manner simply does not work for them. Instead, they need a gradual introduction of appropriately worded personal affirmations, possibly working in harmony with other self-help strategies.

## Time Issue

Sometimes, we start out with the best of intentions; we're all fired up to encompass affirmations into our daily routine, but then find they just don't get done. Life gets in the way, we're too busy, and we didn't give them the attention they need. Positive affirmations need to be practiced for long enough that they have time to reprogram new pathways in our mind and to establish new, self-supporting habits and beliefs.

## Too Many

If we try and change too many things at once, or try and focus on too many things, then we reduce the likelihood of them all being effective. Your mind will struggle with the overload of information, and resist change. Selecting the most important areas in which you desire change, and focusing on them intently, will massively increase your chances of success. As you then become successful in that area of your life, you can then move on to the next area you would like to positively influence.

## Lacking Power

If your affirmations are not powerful enough, or you are not motivated enough to create change in that area of your life, then you won't bother to keep saying them. Stating *'I am wealthy and an abundance of money is all around Me.'* may not be motivational to you if your underlying desire is to find more love and friendship in your life. You need to work on the areas where you are passionate about realizing change. If you are seeking love, then statements such as *'I am a loving person, worthy of finding a special relationship'* or *'Today, I move closer toward finding real love'* will be far more powerful for you, and your brain will respond accordingly, to identify opportunities to support your goals.

## Unrealistic

As with any area in which you seek change, you also need to be realistic about the outcome. If you state *'I am the greatest Formula One racing driver'* when, in reality, you can't drive and have no experience in that area, your chances of succeeding are remote. If you have a goal to lose weight, then personal statements that help you along the journey will be far easier to believe, and to feel positive about, than starting with the end goal of *'I am X lbs'*. When your mind thinks the statement is unrealistic, or unachievable, it will resist the change and not help you move forward. By breaking your personal statements into realistic stages, such as *'Today, I am lighter than yesterday, and tomorrow I will be even lighter,'* or *'I only eat nourishing, healthy foods,'* you will find it much more achievable than a massive mental jump to the end goal. Unrealistic affirmations are hard to stick to whereas realistic ones can make a huge difference.

## Choice of Words

> *"Better than a thousand hollow words, \
> is one word that brings peace."*
> ~ *Buddha*

If your affirmations are not set effectively then they may not work well for you. In the above section on **'Types of Affirmations'**, we looked at the different styles you can select from. A statement of *'I am healthy,'* may not be right for you, if it doesn't resonate well or feel believable, whereas saying *'I am learning to eat healthy, nutritional foods that support my body's needs,'* may produce a more emotionally engaged response from you, and feel good. Think about the specific choice of words for your personal statements, and you will find ones that fit well with your goals, and that your subconscious is happy to embrace.

As you can see, affirmations can fail for various reasons. If you have previously struggled, or are currently struggling, to make them work for you, start with asking yourself, *'Do I believe what I am saying?'* If not, change the statement, so you can commit to something that feels good. It's extremely important for you to believe in the potential of the statement. You could also ask yourself, *'Am I really motivated to see change in this area of my life?'* If your desire is not strong enough, go back and discover what it *really is* that you seek to change, and inject some passion into your statement.

## *Replace Negative Thoughts*

*"Seemingly insignificant choices are like seemingly trivial seeds. Once planted, they root and grow and spread into something tremendous. Imagine the prickly weeds some choices amount to over time and be careful not to plant them."*
*~ Richelle E. Goodrich*

Having too many negative thoughts can cause a whole host of problems. They can hold us back, make us fearful, feel miserable or depressed, keep us stuck in the past, make us hard to be around, and lower our physical and mental resistance to life. Although some negative thoughts are only natural, and are part of who we are (especially if we've had a really bad day!) they should not be what we spend most of our time and energy on.

You may find yourself focusing on thoughts that result in self-doubt, fear, self-limiting beliefs, blame, negativity, moodiness, withdrawal from others, and low self-esteem or low confidence levels. Negative self-talk and poor self-belief can prevent you from being open to enjoy life, can block your ability to move forward, and can lead to stress, poor health, and even depression.

Fortunately, positive affirmations can provide an opportunity to swap, or block, many of these negative thoughts. You can specifically target an area you know is causing you problems, and strengthen your inner positive voice, so that it speaks louder and louder, drowning out, and then replacing, the harmful messages. With repeated use, and the power of your subconscious, you will be able to override the toxic messages, and replace them with a new set of positive beliefs.

*"Once you replace negative thoughts with positive ones, you'll start having positive results."*
*~ Willie Nelson*

Obviously this is not always as easy as it sounds, as you may need to work hard on the reprogramming of your mind, especially if you have deep seated negative beliefs that have been built up over a lifetime. Positive affirmations are not necessarily the complete answer; however, they can be a significant part of the solution.

Start the process by identifying your negative beliefs and internal head chatter. Take time to listen to yourself. Spend a day really focusing on all your thoughts. Are they positive, negative, or neutral? Which ones do you hear most often? How often do they pop up? Are subconscious *negative* affirmations a significant part of your day, without you even realizing it?

**Any of these familiar?**

- It could only happen to me.
- I hate my appearance.
- I'm no good at this.
- Another bad start to the day.
- Why do I ever bother?
- I'm so rubbish at this.
- Nothing good ever comes of my efforts.
- I'm an idiot.
- I've always been too short/tall/thin/fat.
- Why can't I get a break?
- I'll never get past this problem.
- I'd do more if only I wasn't so tired/unfit/poorly/busy/fed up.

Constant self-talk that puts you down or holds you back will hamper your ability, or even desire, to move forward. **Recognize how often you say such words to yourself, and reflect on the power those words have on how you feel about yourself, and your future.** What effect are they having on your life, and how much do you want to alter those thoughts?

Although you can't just flick a switch and stop those thoughts, you can devise techniques to replace the negative phrases, with positive, empowering ones.

| Negative Statement | Positive Statement |
|---|---|
| I'm so stupid. | I enjoy learning new lessons. I will learn from mistakes and welcome all new forms of learning. |
| I'm too unhealthy. | I value my health, and am making wellness my top priority. |
| I always feel unwell/tired/stressed. | I am ready to be healthy and to feel good. I act in the best interests of my body. |
| I don't deserve happiness. | I deserve happiness. I have the right to be happy, healthy and fulfilled. |
| Why do I always do that? | I willingly release old negative habits, and build new, empowering ones instead. |
| I wish my pain would go away. | The pain is lessening every day. My body is healing, and I am well. |
| I don't feel comfortable meeting new people. | I'm strong and confident. I welcome the opportunity to meet interesting new people. |

| | |
|---|---|
| I'm rubbish at this. | I know this is a challenge, and I'll learn positive things from it, while I work to find a solution. |
| I'm too afraid to let someone new into my life. | Today, I release fear and open my heart to love. |
| Another horrible start to the day. | Today will be a good day. I will quickly move past any problems and expect only good things to occur for the rest of the day. |

Swapping negative thoughts for positive ones is not an overnight process. However, with time and practice you *will* find that your thoughts begin to automatically appear as positive, affirming statements rather than the previously held negative ones. If you do find you've slipped back into bad thinking habits, take time out, and specifically focus on counteracting negative statements with positive ones.

*"Knowledge is two-fold, and consists not only in an affirmation of what is true, but in the negation of that which is false."*
*~ Charles Caleb Colton*

The words we choose have an amazingly strong influence over our moods and actions. Combine positive statements, such as the examples above, along with personal affirmations, such as *'I choose to be happy,'* or *'My life is a blessing,'* and you will empower yourself to achieve so much more.

Swapping negative thoughts for positive, self-affirming ones is an effective method for moving your mindset to happier place. **Build awareness, be brave and believe in yourself!**

## *Stuck In A Rut*

> *"He who is not courageous enough*
> *to take risks will accomplish*
> *nothing in life."*
> *~ Muhammad Ali*

One of the main reasons for using positive affirmations is to help you move forward, and proactively change a bad or static situation. When you have an area of your life that is stagnating, or you are dissatisfied with, then a specifically targeted affirmation, coupled with relevant actions, can work wonders.

**Examples of areas you may be stuck in:**

- You don't think you have the ability to be promoted.
- You're bored with your job and prospects.
- You think weight loss is too hard.
- You are stuck in a loveless relationship.
- You're fed up with your appearance and clothes, but don't know how to change.
- Nothing good ever happens.
- Your social life is non-existent.
- Money is always tight.

You can use positive affirmations to drive change that can affect both your attitude *and* your situation. When you are stuck in rut, you need to actively change the things you *do* to experience a difference. Positive affirmations, combined with energy and determination, will take you to a whole new place.

## *Take Control*

Positive affirmations allow us to take control of our thoughts and actions. More importantly, they enable us to take personal responsibility for how we feel.

**You have the freedom to choose how you think about something.** You may currently have preconditioned negative thoughts about a certain subject; however, these thoughts can be altered and replaced with a positive mindset.

You create stress and tension in your body when you say statements such as:

- *'I can't'*
- *'I'll fail'*
- *'I'll never achieve that'*
- *'I hate xxx'*
- *'No-one cares'*
- *'I'm too stupid'*

However, when you use words such as '*I can, I am, I love, I'm smart enough to do X'*, then you have taken control, and have exerted power over your negative emotions. By using positive affirmations with uplifting words, you can automatically feel calmer and more in control. For example, if you are about to deliver a presentation to your co-workers, saying, *'I am calm, I am in control, and I am about to deliver a great presentation,'* feels so much more empowering than *'I'm so stressed, this will be awful, I'm going to embarrass myself'*.

We can allow our fears and worries to control us, or we can take control of *them*. The use of positive affirmations and positive self-talk can help transform our lives, as they provide us with a sense of control and power over situations. A simple change in the words we permit ourselves to use can make the world of difference.

An additional benefit to using positive affirmations is that they can allow us to direct our focus toward a specific target, increasing our productivity and, therefore, our chances of success. If you want to become fit and train for a half marathon, then positive affirmations will help support your goals. Daily affirmations that focus on health, fitness and relevant training activities will help to ensure your mind is engaged in supportive thoughts, and focus it on seeking out opportunities to get you closer to your goal.

Positive affirmations are an important part of controlling how we feel, plus what actions we take can consequently transform our thinking patterns for good.

## *Success Making*

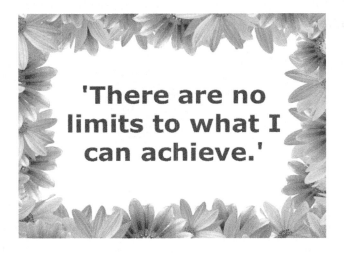

'There are no
limits to what I
can achieve.'

*"Whatever the mind can conceive and believe,*
*the mind can achieve."*
*~ Napoleon Hill*

Everyone wants to be a success in life. Whether it's in love, at work, as a homemaker, in health, or in happiness. Success means different things to different people. For some, it could mean overcoming a fear, and for others, conquering a new challenge or material or personal gain.

The use of success affirmations can program your mind to expect success, and to support you in your efforts toward your intended goal. They can help to focus your energy on being productive, to select the most beneficial activities, and help you to maximize your own potential.

You will, however, need to set your mind to *expect* success. Plus, you are most likely to achieve success in areas you care about the most. To be successful with something, you need to be:

- Passionate about it.

- Resilient to a few knock backs along the way.

- Committed to doing whatever it takes to make it happen.

If your desire, motivation, or commitment level is weak, you will struggle to make progress. If you think the goal is unachievable then your mind will also shy away from any efforts to support you. To be successful in the areas you care about, you need to know the outcome in achievable, and believe that you are capable of making it happen. This is where success affirmations play their part:

- *'I have within me the power to succeed.'*

- *'I celebrate my successes every day.'*

- *'My life is good and I am thankful for my success, which increases every day.'*

Having the intention of a successful outcome means you are setting an expectation in your mind of being successful. Using words such as '*I can, I am, I have, I allow, I expect*' in combination with positive statements, embeds the thoughts and expectations into your subconscious. This, is turn, will influence your conscious thinking, and the positive actions you take to move toward your goal.

## *Provides Strength*

The use of positive affirmations can be an effective way of building up your mental strength, your resistance to problems and your ability to overcome issues that hold you back. They can give you the strength to fight health problems, to be creative, to seek solutions, tackle emotional problems, and so forth. Overall, they are a powerful tool for improving your general well-being.

Anyone who suffers with issues of self-esteem, or low confidence, knows how debilitating they can be. Building up your personal resources and improving your sense of self-worth can make an incredible difference to your life. Improvements in your self-esteem and confidence means you are more likely to cope with stress, failure, rejection, loss, health problems, and everyday issues much more easily. Self-esteem affirmations focus on recognizing your personal value, and can help to build strength in areas you feel vulnerable:

- *'I have confidence in myself and my ability to achieve whatever I want.'*
- *'I am kind and supportive, and enjoy doing good things for others.'*
- *'I am perfectly okay as I am. I fully accept and love myself.'*
- *'I live my life with courage and optimism.'*
- *'I accept myself unconditionally. I don't need others' approval, just to know I've done my best.'*
- *'I am unique and blessed to be alive.'*

Strength based affirmations can help to counteract negative thoughts, and the harmful effects of negative self-belief. We know these can be destructive and harmful to our well-being, so focusing on strength-based affirmations can help us to move in a positive direction, develop in areas we seek growth, and build strength in areas of insecurity.

- *'I am strong in the face of negative influences.'*
- *'I love life and face it head on, with courage and enthusiasm.'*
- *'I believe in myself and my ability to achieve.'*

Affirmations that are inspiring, uplifting and healing will give us an important boost in the areas where we need it. **Who wouldn't want to use a simple tool to inspire, uplift, and heal?**

## *Benefits Others*

When you are the best you can be, you add extra value to those you care about.

By tackling our insecurities, fears, doubts, and emotional issues, we strengthen ourselves, and are able to give more to others. If we are crippled by doubts, stuck in the past, fearful of 'what-ifs', or withdrawn from relationships, then we are not giving anywhere near the best of ourselves to others, or to ourselves.

Positive affirmations, possibly in combination with other self-help tools, enable us to tackle these issues. We can then give more of ourselves, and benefit others in various ways. **For example:**

- Confidence issues may have kept you out of the dating arena, and yet someone is missing out on your ability to love them.
- Fitness levels may have held you back from enjoying sporting activities with your children.
- Health worries may have kept you away from social activities with friends.

- Low self-esteem may have stopped you from applying for promotion, so your employer misses out on your skills and ability.

Take control of these issues, and you will allow yourself to move forward, enjoy life more, and add huge value to those around you. **Try creating statements such as:**

- *'I help others when I help myself.'*
- *'I feel energized when I do my best and can help others.'*
- *'I bring out the best in others when I bring out the best in me.'*

## *Feel Good About Yourself*

The purpose of positive affirmations is to enable your thoughts and emotions to move to a healthy, happy place, allowing you to feel more contented, confident, open, optimistic, and empowered to achieve so much more with your life.

> *"When I feel good about myself, things start happening for myself.
> When you look up, you go up."*
> *~ Herschel Walker*

Emotions that sap your strength, and cause conflict, stress, and anxiety are bad for you in so many ways. Not least, they *feel* bad. No one wants to live with fear, blame, guilt, disappointment, bitterness, shame, or self-doubt. Struggling against negative emotions can take up a lot of time and energy – both of which you could use to far better effect elsewhere in your life.

Breaking the chains of negative baggage means you can move forward with your life and start to feel good. Holding on to old issues and self-doubt blocks you from allowing good things into your life. Fortunately, you have the choice to change. As hard as it may seem at times, especially if you have suffered a lifetime of negative thoughts, it is possible, and absolutely worth the effort.

The more often you repeat something to yourself, the more you will start to believe it. Providing you are using positive self-talk that does not cause your subconscious to raise a flag of resistance, then you are choosing to reprogram your mind with positivity. Positive affirmations help to imprint new self-affirming pathways into your subconscious, replacing the self-defeating messages you were previously hearing. These new pathways will then start to help you to feel good about yourself:

- *'My body is full of healthy, healing, positive energy.'*
- *'I respect myself for who I am.'*

- *'I let go of negativity and focus only on positive thoughts.'*

If you find yourself slipping back into a place of negativity, stress or self-doubt, introduce some positive affirmations that will help you to feel good again. Notice what works well for you, which words resonate strongly with you, and make you feel positive, excited, uplifted, in control, or powerful.

- *'I have the power to control my health and happiness.'*
- *'I am free to choose.'*
- *'I feel happy, optimistic, and in control.'*
- *'I am open to allowing love into my life.'*
- *'Today is going to be a 'feel good' day.'*

Positive affirmations are a great tool for quickly getting your mindset back to a place of positivity, and focusing you on 'feel good' thoughts and actions.

## 4

## How To Use Them Effectively

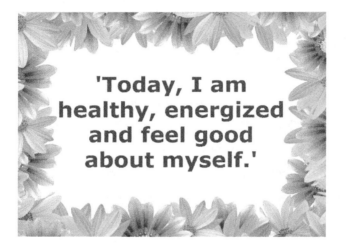

'Today, I am healthy, energized and feel good about myself.'

*"Our thoughts are so precious.*
*Every thought we think is creating our future."*
*~ Louise Hay*

Learning to use positive affirmations will provide you with a powerful method to change your life, grow in new directions and heal old wounds. Unfortunately, although they can be simple and easy to carry out, they can also be easy to get wrong. If they are incorrectly used, you may feel they have failed, and therefore stop trying to use them. However, effectively executed affirmations can supercharge your life in so many ways, ways that are exciting, empowering, and completely life changing. **These positive changes can lead to better mental and physical health, and an overall sense of well-being and happiness.**

The trick is to find the styles and wording that work best for you, and to use them in the most effective manner possible. Then, you will experience some amazing results.

## *The Need For Effective Methods*

### Working with the subconscious

Positive affirmations work by targeting our beliefs at a subconscious level. Therefore, they need to be believable, in order for our mind to accept them. For example, if you say *'I am the world's fittest person'*, your mind will reject that thought as being untrue. Whereas, if you say, *'I am becoming the fittest possible version of myself'*, then your subconscious will accept this fact, and support your desire to move in that direction. An affirmation is far more likely to work effectively, when you avoid internal resistance. Your subconscious is not easily fooled; therefore, you need to provide it with statements it's comfortable to work with.

It's also likely that your mind will be resistant to change. Deep seated fears and negative self-beliefs can be hard to change, and so the methods required to alter these thoughts and feelings need to be appropriately selected for the task. **The subconscious responds not just to the words we say, but also the images we feed it, and the feelings we associate with certain thoughts or experiences.** Combining positive affirmations with other methods such as visualization and meditation can be a powerful approach, allowing us to successfully steer our subconscious in the direction we want it to go. The effective use of these types of methods can override previously embedded negative beliefs, by implanting fresh massages of health, well-being, and success.

*"Only one thing registers on the subconscious mind: repetitive application – practice.*
*What you practice is what you manifest."*
*~ Fay Weldon*

**Positive, Present Tense, and Personal**
The most effective affirmations will follow the rule of being positive, set in the present, and personal to you. Positive statements encourage your mind to work *toward* achieving something good, as opposed to having to move *away* from something negative. Instead of saying *'I am not shy'*, state *'I am confident and open to*

*meeting new people.'* Your subconscious will respond to a positive statement by setting a new pathway for that belief, whereas giving it an instruction to not focus on 'being shy' means it will automatically focus on the shy element, reinforcing the feelings you have around being shy.

Setting your affirmations in the present tense allows your subconscious to accept the statement as true (as long as it is also believable). If you have been feeling unwell, stating *'I will feel healthy at some point soon',* is no-where near as powerful as stating *'I am feeling good today, and my health improves more and more each day',* or *'Today is a good day, my body is healing and I am well.'*

Affirmations should always be personal to you. You cannot control how others feel or act; however, you can control what's specific to you. Your subconscious will only operate at a level that's controlled to you. If you state *'Alex will be healthy'* you are stating a wish or a hope for someone else, which you have little control over. Whereas, if you state *'I support Alex in becoming healthy',* then you are able to control the intent of this statement, and, therefore, act accordingly. Affirmation statements also need to work for you at a level you are comfortable with. If you state *'I am happy',* when you feel miserable, then your subconscious will reject this as being untrue. A personal statement you may react better to could be *'My life is moving in a happier direction',* or *'I am learning to focus on happy thoughts.'* It's important that you feel personally connected to the affirmation statement, for it to work effectively.

**Get Emotional**

When you use emotionally powerful words, you will evoke certain feelings, which make it easier to embed the positive thoughts into your subconscious. Words such as *'joy, fun, happy, exciting, love, passion, desire, power,'* can cause you to feel the corresponding emotion, when said with conviction. Combine this with the use of visualization, and you can conjure up many positive thoughts and feelings to associate with your personal affirmations.

*"Visualize this thing that you want, see it, feel it, believe in it. Make your mental blue print, and begin to build."*
*~ Robert Collier*

When you craft a strong, meaningful personal belief statement, and are committed to the process of change, then you will be using a highly effective method for creating your optimal future. If you want to create the feeling of being calm and relaxed, or being excited and powerful, then give your subconscious something relevant to work with.

Choose the words that resonate with your desire, and use your imagination to conjure up related images, and you'll soon be on your way to having those thoughts and feelings automatically pop up in your life.

The section below, on *'Understanding The Power of Words',* explores this subject in more detail.

**Amplify The Feelings**
Amplify your chances of success by ensuring your mind is set to a positive position when you say your affirmations. Words alone are not sufficient to create the changes you seek. Even if you have created a highly targeted personal affirmation, it will have little impact if you say it while feeling negative.

For example, if you are feeling down, or unwell, or generally out of sorts, it can be hard to shake these feelings. Repeating a positive affirmation while feeling bad, will only highlight the fact that you are feeling bad, and your subconscious will then associate the affirmation with bad feelings. This will block them from working effectively.

Therefore, you need to find a way to inject positivity into *how* you say the words. Stand up tall, relax your shoulders, take a few deep breaths, smile (into a mirror if possible), and say your affirmations in a positive tone. Your subconscious doesn't differentiate between a real smile and a purposely created smile. Conjure up a memory or thought of something that makes you feel good, and hold those feelings tightly as you state your affirmations. Your subconscious will associate the

49

positive statement with the happy feelings, and, therefore, the statement automatically becomes believable and far more effective.

Positive affirmations, when used regularly, will weaken and replace old negative beliefs, enabling you to move forward. The effective use of affirmations means they become an automatic part of your thought processes. You will, therefore, be strengthening your level of self-worth, building self-esteem, and freeing yourself to feel happier and healthier.

We'll discuss further steps to enhance their effectiveness in the sections below.

## *Use Them Correctly*

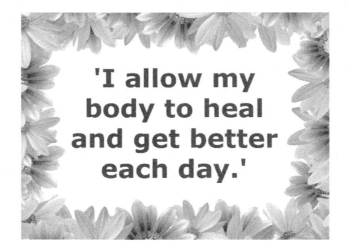

'I allow my body to heal and get better each day.'

Affirmations will only be effective when used correctly. There are various techniques that allow you to enhance your chances of success; however, it's important to make sure they are designed to suit your personal style, and preferred methods.

To receive the best results from your positive affirmations, check that they meet the following criteria:

- **Adaptable, to suit your personal style** – if you try and force a method or technique you are not comfortable with, you will likely stop doing it. Finding a method that fits comfortably with your lifestyle, and that your mind does not resist, is a key factor in ensuring the effectiveness of your affirmations.

- **Fit easily into your daily schedule** – identify the best times for you to say your personal affirmations. This could be before you get out of bed, in the bathroom mirror before work, when commuting to work, your lunch break, before going to bed, and so on. There will be certain times when you find them easier to do, and when you find them to be the most powerful.

- **Are realistic** – don't expect miracles too quickly, or set the bar too high. Make sure your statements are believable. Keep them short and simple.

- **Stated in the first person** – Keep them personal to you, e.g. *'I am, I can, I intend...'*

- **Action-oriented and strong** – Focus on positive, strengthening statements and avoid weak or negative phrases such as *'I'll try, maybe, I might, I'll avoid...'*

- **Stated in the present** – create your statement in the present, don't forward project. For example, *'I am calm'* as opposed to *'I will be calm after the presentation.'*

- **Powerful** – your personal affirmations should evoke powerful positive emotions when you state them. They should be designed to elicit feelings such as peace, happiness, strength, power, confidence, decisiveness, control, etc.

- **Repeated** – if rarely used, they are unlikely to be effective. Build them into your daily routine, so you can create empowering new affirmations habits. These will eventually become part of your automatic thought processes, and need less active planning.

The correct use of positive affirmations requires the right choice of affirmations in the first place, the use of powerful words, combined with effective techniques, and the appropriate frequency. Get these right and you are well on your way to creating the mindset and lifestyle you desire.

## *Make The Time*

Take some time to consider what areas of your life you want to improve, and which areas to prioritize. If you have various aspects of your life in which you would like to affect change, pick the ones that are most important to start with.

Like anything worthwhile in life, you will need to create the time to work on them, and to give them the focus they deserve.

You may find that there are certain times of the day when you have more time or energy to dedicate to them. You may naturally gravitate toward a certain time block, or you may find you like to practice them throughout the day, when you have a few moments:

- Early morning, so you set a positive tone for the day
- When you walk or commute somewhere, so you utilize the time wisely
- In the shower or bath, so you're relaxed and able to focus

- Bedtime, so your mind is focused on your desired outcome, as you drift off to sleep

The use of prompts can be helpful, as you build the new habit of daily positive affirmations. You could use items such as a daily journal, images stuck to the bathroom mirror, affirmation statements in your wallet, or a poster that represents your desires.

Try to set up a routine for your affirmations, so that you are less likely to become caught up in all your other daily to-dos. Make your affirmations a priority, either by setting aside a specific time to practice them, or by having various prompts around you, which act as reminders throughout the day.

It's also relevant to remember that once you start to see positive results in a specific area of your life, you are likely to stop using the positive affirmations to support it. However, if at some point in the future that area starts to cause you concern again, then make the time to re-engage with your personal positive statements, and put yourself back in control.

There is no set timescale in which affirmations are expected to work. Their ability to help you bring about positive change in your life can depend on the depth of the issue you are dealing with. If you are committed to the process of change, and are using a combination of highly effective techniques, then change can happen quickly. As with most things though, the use of affirmations takes time and effort. Regardless of the timescale, the potential benefits are well worth the effort.

## *Different Techniques*

There are various techniques you can use to support your affirmations statements. Your choice may depend upon what you are comfortable with, how much time you want to invest, and what time you realistically have available each day.   Combining these techniques can work extremely well, and will provide you with a greater opportunity for each technique to work its wonders.

**Example techniques:**

**Visualization**
As the famous quote goes, *'Seeing is believing'*. Visualizing your desired outcome in all its glorious detail is a powerful way to communicate with your subconscious. Take time out to let your imagination take over. Create images in your mind as to how things will be once you have achieved your goal – how do things look, smell, taste, sound? What emotions are you experiencing? Totally immerse yourself in the details of the moment.

Your subconscious will accept those images, and help you to recognize, and be open to, receiving new ideas, opportunities, resources, and people into your life, all of which support your desires. Plus, when you 'experience' the fabulous benefits of your desired outcome, you'll be more motivated and inspired to take action to get yourself to that place of reality.

You may need to practice the art of visualization to begin with, however, when you have created compelling images for where you want to be, who or how you'd like to be, who you'd like to be with , and so forth, you'll be able to conjure up those images any time you like. Create those inspired moments whenever you need a mental boost, or reminder as to why your affirmations are important.

*"To accomplish great things we must first dream,*
*then visualize, then plan... believe... act!"*
*~ Alfred A. Montapert*

## Meditation

The use of meditation can be a highly effective technique when linked to your personal affirmations. Meditation gives your mind a chance to slow down, giving you the opportunity to relax, to find a sense of peace, and to find mental clarity where you need it.

Regular meditation allows you to tune into the deeper and more influential areas of your mind. As your conscious mind slows down, and is permitted to take a break from the constant bombardment of thoughts, your subconscious mind is allowed to take over. You can completely focus on embedding your positive new affirmation beliefs deep into your subconscious, thus creating a potent combination of techniques.

There are various ways to practice meditation, which are beyond the scope of this book. However, there are numerous books and information available on the Internet, which can get you started, and enable you to become skilled at the practice of meditation. Make sure to take some time to meditate prior to making your affirmations statements.

**You could link your affirmations to your meditation sessions in ways such as:**

- Focus on a specific word e.g. health, peace, healing, abundance, happiness, etc.
- Focus on an important positive affirmation, repeating it many times e.g. *'I am well'*.
- Focus on a mental image of your desired outcome, associate it with positive feelings, and hold onto the image. Also, state your positive affirmation words while linking to the image.
- Listen to guided meditation audio recordings.

Effective meditation takes time and patience. Unfortunately, your conscious mind won't easily let go of the surging thoughts it has swirling around. However, it *is* possible to control your mind, and enable it to support your goals. Eventually, you will be able to meditate easily, and without the need for much preparation. You will then be able to take a few minutes each day, or as often as required, to focus on meditating with your positive affirmations.

**Mirror Work**

Another powerful technique can be to practice your affirmations in front of a mirror. This is a technique often noted, although should be adapted to a style you are comfortable with.

**Benefits of mirror work and affirmations:**

- You have a private space and moment to yourself.

- You can look yourself in the eye and state your personal affirmations with conviction.

- Link to other habits – cleaning teeth, brushing hair, washing hands, etc. Take an extra moment to reiterate your affirmations to yourself.

- Helps to embed the new belief into your subconscious.

- You can observe your body language and responses to each affirmations statement. You can alter your posture, facial expression and tone of voice to ensure you are stating your affirmations in the best possible way.

**Methods of Mirror Work:**

- Start your day right – for example, state '*Today will be a good day*' or '*I am healthy and strong today*' into the mirror as you begin your day. Repeat at least ten times.

- Smile at yourself in the mirror, think positive thoughts, and imbue your affirmations with a sense of positivity.

- Tell negative thoughts to go away – actively state that you let them go, and repeat a positive affirmation to replace it. State '*I let go of a poor body image'*, and then state *'I feel confident and happy with who I am.'*

- Stand up tall, and be confident. Relax and breathe slowly in/out for five breaths. Slowly and confidently state your personal affirmations.

Practicing your affirmations in front of a mirror may feel awkward at first; however, with a bit of practice, you'll soon experience the benefits, and reap the rewards.

## Write It Down

Writing down your affirmations helps you to retain focus. Creating a list of affirmations can also be linked to journal writing or a gratitude diary. Repeatedly reading your affirmations helps to embed them onto your subconscious, and can inspire you to act in ways that actively support your desired outcome.

Taking time to write your affirmations out on a daily basis is another technique for installing positive new self-beliefs onto your subconscious, and keeping them front of mind.

## See It Clearly

Daily life can get annoyingly busy for most of us; therefore having visual prompts to remind us of our affirmation desires can be extremely helpful. They can be large and unmissable, or discreet and unobtrusive. Examples can include:

- Motivational posters
- Affirmation cards or a calendar
- Photos or inspirational quotes on the bathroom mirror
- Screen saver on your phone
- Inspirational bookmark
- Lucky charm in your wallet
- A bright scarf, socks, trainers, makeup, etc.

It's very easy to become distracted, and before you know it, the day has passed, and you haven't made your positive affirmations. By having visual reminders waving at you as you pass by, or whispering to you discreetly, you'll be reminded to take the time to make your positive statements, without losing a precious day.

## Be Confident and Expect Results

*How* you say your statements is just as important as *why* you're making your positive affirmations. If you make your statements while sounding or feeling unconfident, negative, or without positive belief, you will struggle to get the results you desire.

**Effective techniques for imbuing confidence into your statements could be:**

- Stand or sit up straight
- Smile
- Relax your shoulders and take a few deep breaths
- Fix your mind on positive thoughts
- Visualize your desired outcome
- Slowly, and assertively, state your personal affirmations
- Have confidence in your statement (or tweak it until you feel it is believable and you can be confident with it)
- Expect the result you desire

A strong expectation of achieving your goal is an important component. If you repeatedly state an affirmation, yet your internal belief is such that it won't happen, then you will not enjoy a positive outcome. **Having a high expectation of a desired outcome is critical to ensuring the result you want.** Make sure your expectations are aligned correctly.

An effective set of techniques can make the difference between a weak set of affirmations, and a powerful set. However, you need to put these techniques to work on a consistent basis.

**Nothing will change for the better unless you take specific action, and *then* you'll make some great things happen.**

## *Tools*

When we try to install new habits and behaviors we need as much support, encouragement, and helpful reminders as possible. By using the right tools, you can steer yourself toward your desired outcome, with the least amount of effort, and lessen the chances of failure.

**Examples of supportive tools could be:**

### Affirmations Journal

Taking the time to record your thoughts, feelings, and activities each day can be very powerful. The process asks you to reflect on your day, and to understand what worked, and what didn't. It gives you the opportunity to change what isn't working so well, and to do more of what does work. As you practice your affirmation thoughts, you'll become more skilled at using them. Recording your journey in a journal allows you to see how well, and how quickly, you are progressing toward your goal.

## Writing Down Your Thoughts

Capturing your thoughts in writing can help give you clarity. This could take the form of writing a letter to yourself (including a commitment to create change where you want to), writing out a goal list, creating a list of affirmations in priority order, or listing negative thoughts and then replacing them with positive statements.

The act of writing things down helps you to capture what you really want to achieve, and allows you to refer back to your notes whenever you need to refresh, or remind yourself of where you're going.

## Books or Affirmation Cards

Books on affirmations can offer inspiration and helpful prompts. Many will have suggested affirmations you can use, or adapt for your personal use. Some books, cards and calendars offer daily thoughts, which you may find helpful to have on hand.

## Audio

Motivational CDs, or audio recordings, can be a great way to increase your passion for change. They can inspire you, light a fire under you, and put you back on track if you've veered off course. There are many that focus on affirmations, with others that are designed to motivate you in specific areas you are interested in (and that you can then tie into your own personal statements).

## Creative Prompts

Let your creative juices run free, and design some things that stimulate your imagination, and remind you *why* you created your positive affirmations. Develop a vision board, a playlist of inspiring or motivational music, your own vision/affirmations cards, or plant a window box and nurture it as you nurture your new positive thoughts. Create something meaningful, and link it to your affirmation statements.

## Other prompts

If you struggle to remember to practice your affirmations, then you may need to be more direct. Set a daily alarm on your phone, schedule a specific time or place (where you'll see a visual prompt), link it to another daily habit, e.g. as you brush your teeth, or reward yourself with a daily treat once you have completed your affirmations.

## *How Often*

Repetition is the key to learning, to creating new habits and installing fresh, empowering sets of beliefs.

That is not to say that you need to repeat your affirmations thousands of time, or so often that they start to annoy you. The more powerful, and effective the affirmation, the quicker it will work, and the less you will need to actively practice it.

So, how often should you state your positive affirmations? There is no specific right or wrong. However, there are some effective guidelines that work well for many people, in terms of when and how often to make their personal statements:

- At least once a day, for a minimum five minutes.
- Twice per day is even more effective.
- Start the day with a positive focus and clarity of thought.
- Finish the day with reflection, gratitude, and specific statements, so you embed the affirming thoughts into your subconscious overnight.
- Create extra opportunities as they arise – on the bus, stuck in queue, when making coffee, etc.

Consistency is critical. The more you affirm your positive statement, the deeper your subconscious will embed the thought, leading to positive change wherever you direct it. Maintain the practice of using your new belief statements until they naturally feel a part of your mindset. You can then move on to a fresh set of positive affirmations, so you can affect changes elsewhere in your life, or reinstate the original ones, as and when you need them.

## *How Many*

This is a personal choice, and depends on what you intend to change, and the depth of the issues you are tackling.

You may be comfortable with creating change in several areas of your life at the same time, or you may find it more effective to focus on the most important area first, before moving on to the next. It will be easier to see positive changes taking shape in one specific area, which will then give you the confidence, and the belief, to continue using affirmations in other areas of your life.

You could consider grouping a set of affirmations together, which are focused on one key area. For example, you could focus on your health, and use a combination of affirmations:

- *'I feel good today.'*
- *'My body is fit and I am full of energy.'*
- *'I see myself happy and healthy.'*
- *'I love to take good care of myself and others.'*
- *'I allow myself to heal and feel well.'*

If this feels like too much, you could focus on one very specific affirmation, such as *'I take daily steps to ensure my health and happiness',* and then put all your energy and focus into working with this statement.

Alternatively, you could select affirmation statements that focus on several different aspects of your life, such as health, career, confidence building, creativity and so on. However, be careful not to choose too many at once, as you may become overwhelmed, and therefore reduce the likelihood any of your statements will be effective.

Many people find it more effective to focus on specific areas, one at a time. By selecting positive affirmations, with a powerful choice of words, and using them consistently, the impact will be greater than trying to overload yourself with too many at once.

## *Understand The Power Of Words*

Your words are an incredibly powerful tool. Use the wrong ones, and your affirmations won't work (or worse, they will cause a negative effect, compounding any issues you have with self-esteem or negativity).

For an affirmation to be effective, it needs to evoke strong emotions and desire. If you make a statement that does not ring true, then your subconscious will reject it. However, if you change the words to make the statement believable, then your subconscious will easily accept it, and actively help you achieve it.

## Choose your words carefully, as they can have a lasting impact.

### Eliminate

There is no place in positive affirmations for negative, weak, or hesitant words. Remove any words such as *'don't, won't, can't, may be, possibly, try, stop, have a go, am planning, never'*, and so forth. You may find that you use some of these words out of habit; however, you need to find positive alternatives for your personal affirmations to be effective. Don't let negative words near your personal statements.

*"You're only as weak as you let yourself become, and you're only as strong as you allow yourself to be."*
*~ Daniel Hansen*

## Strengthen

If an affirmation feels wrong, for example, when you say *'I am healthy'*, yet you clearly feel unwell, your mind will dismiss it. However, if you enhance the statement with words such as *'I choose, I accept, I am prepared, I am open to'*, you create a more authentic statement. Saying, *'I am ready to be healthy'*, is more empowering and believable, and encourages you to focus on health giving actions.

## Enhance

You can also remove doubt from your mind when you add supportive words to your statements. If you find saying *'I am healthy and happy'* to cause resistance in your mind, use statements such as *'I am learning to, I become better and better each day, my health is improving daily, and I gain new knowledge every day'*.

You can influence your subconscious in both positive and negative ways. Careful selection of your words enables you to influence it to your advantage, which can lead to great improvements in both your emotional and physical health and well-being. Practice using empowering, uplifting, enabling words often enough, and you'll successfully create lasting, positive change in your life.

## *Link To Gratitude*

'I am
grateful
to be me.'

**Demonstrating gratitude for the good things
in your life is a healthy habit from which
you can reap many benefits.**

Take time each day to actively give thanks for your
health, loved ones, freedom to choose, financial security,
knowledge, friends, and so on.

Or, maybe just recognize and be thankful for small
enjoyments such as a pleasant meal, time spent reading
a good book, or a sunny afternoon.

**People who regularly express gratitude are generally:**

- More optimistic
- Healthier as a result of better immune systems
- More proactive about health and wellness
- Less stressed
- Feel better about themselves

**Affirmations can be linked to gratitude in a couple of ways:**

## Combined

You can express your gratitude for the new experiences and opportunities that have arrived in your life already, or are about to arrive. If you practice daily gratitude thoughts, be sure to include all the movement you have seen or felt toward your personal affirmation statement. If your affirmation statement is *'I give myself permission to relax and heal without any guilt'*, then give thanks at the end of the day for time you have given to resting, actions you've taken toward healing, helpful information you've received, or people who have helped you.

## Separate

Gratitude statements can be positive affirmations in their own right. You can use the healthy energy of gratitude to boost your affirmations, to attract more of what you want, and to have greater impact on your affirmation efforts. **For example:**

- *'I am blessed in so many ways.'*
- *'I am grateful for this sunny morning as it makes everyone feel cheerful.'*
- *'I am thankful for the loving, caring people I have in my life.'*
- *'The more I am grateful, the more I see to be grateful for.'*
- *'I expect to be healthy and happy, and am grateful for every opportunity to be so.'*

The more you practice giving daily thanks, the more you will notice to be thankful for.

> *Gratitude is riches.*
> *Complain is poverty.*
> *~ Doris Day*

Allow the positive energy to flow into you, and be mindful of everything you have to be grateful for, in the past, present, and future. **Link your positive affirmations to your gratitude habits, and you have a winning combination.**

## *Affirmation Habits*

*"Even the smallest changes in our daily routine
can create incredible ripple effects that
expand our vision of what is possible."*
*~Charles F. Glassman*

Much of our behavior is driven from habits we have formed over time. Learning to incorporate affirmation habits into your daily routine is a highly beneficial process.

Well-crafted personal affirmations can help to break destructive habits, and build new, healthy, supportive ones. Fortunately, with around 3-4 weeks' worth of daily practice, new habits can be installed into your memory bank. They will then fall naturally into your daily routines, becoming familiar in the same way as brushing your hair in the morning, or putting on your shoes as you leave the house.

However, the breaking of bad habits can often be problematic. The time and effort required may be down to how deeply embedded the habit is, and how motivated you are to change it. Fortunately, there are methods available for replacing negative, self-destructive habits with new self-empowering ones. Self-affirming statements and behaviors are one of the strongest techniques you can use to release and replace negative habits.

## Examples of supportive self affirming statements:

- *'Today I choose to let go of my negative habits/s.'*
- *'It feels great to take control of my life and to make choices based on my own health and happiness.'*
- *'I replace self-limiting habits with empowering, nurturing ones.'*
- *'I have conquered the habit of X.'*
- *'I maintain healthy, helpful habits every day, and I am proud of myself.'*

The building of positive affirmation habits means you are programming your mind to release patterns of bad behavior, and develop natural, healthy habits instead. These, in turn, can have a huge impact on your levels of self-esteem and overall happiness.

## *Boost Their Power*

*"When you assess your own life, consider it with the eye of a gardener. Underneath the surface lies rich, fertile soil waiting to nurture the seeds you sow. Even more than you can imagine will grow there if given a chance."*
~ *Steve Goodier*

As we've seen in earlier chapters, affirmations are powerful instruments for fueling positive change. We've looked at a number of effective techniques, such as visualization, meditation, writing your affirmations down, mirror work, and so on, to ensure they achieve the results you desire. Now, we'll look at some extra tips to boost their power even further.

## Inject Passion

Ignite your imagination, and evoke as many positive feelings as possible. Think about past experiences where you have felt relaxed and carefree, where you've had fun with friends and laughed until it hurt, or felt warm and comfortable. Picture your goal in vivid detail, and really feel the intensity of the moment. Then, when you repeat your affirmations, enjoy the sense of excitement you've carried over from your mental image, and let the positive energy wash through you.

## Recognize Your Feelings

Both your mind and body will give you feedback if your affirmation statements are working for you or not. If you do not believe an affirmation as you say or think it, your mind will create a barrier, resist it, or outright reject it (and you may well hear some blunt rebuttals). Your body will join in by tensing up, feeling uncomfortable, and you may even see the rejection on your face.

On the other hand, when your statements are believable, empowering and nurturing, you will feel a sense of calm acceptance, and positive energy. When your statements make you feel optimistic and excited for the day, you know you are getting it right.

## Only Affirm What You Really Want

Understand your true motivations. Your initial 'goal' may not be the one you should be focusing on. For example, you set a goal to lose weight, so you can fit into your skinny jeans. However, your true motivations are to feel confident and outgoing; therefore, your focus should be on confidence building.

Although weight loss may be a factor in helping you to feel more confident, your affirmation statements will be more effective if they are aimed at improving your overall confidence levels. Once you understand what you *really* want, you can structure your affirmations and actions accordingly.

## Chant, Sing, or Hum Your Affirmations

Although this may not feel comfortable for everyone, it can be a great way to reinforce your affirmations. Remember how catchy certain adverts or song choruses can be? Once they're in your head, they often stick around, repeating themselves over and over.

In the same way, you can create your own theme tune for each affirmation. Sing them out loud, and be proud. Or, hum them silently to yourself. Choose whichever works well for you.

## Smile

Give your affirmations a major boost by smiling as you say them, or think about them. Even a fake smile can have the effect of improving your mood and lowering stress levels. An added bonus is that your subconscious will associate the feel good vibes directly with your personal affirmations.

And then there's the powerful effect of laughter, which releases endorphins, one of natures 'feel good' hormones. And, of course, smiling and laughing makes us more attractive to other people, nicer to be around, and can be contagious. **Who doesn't want to be around someone happy and smiling?**

## Link To Gratitude

We mentioned the importance of gratitude in an earlier section. By actively thinking about the things you have received into your life each day, especially when relevant to your daily affirmations, you give them more power. This process helps you to clearly see how well you are progressing. Plus, when you give thanks for the things you have not yet received, you are helping to attract them into your life, and you will be ready and open to receiving them when they appear.

**Be Flexible**

You may feel comfortable having a single statement you repeat each day, which you practice until it is effective. Or, you may prefer to mix up your statements, using different *categories, styles,* and **words**. There may be some days when certain statements feel more relevant, as a result of circumstances, or how you feel. Be flexible, mix and match if it works for you, and do what feels right.

The above superchargers are some great examples of steps you can take toward achieving what you really want through the power of affirmations. Consistent daily actions, which help to program your subconscious into believing new and empowering thoughts, will increase the potency of those thoughts immensely.

*Live your beliefs and you can turn the world around.*
*~ Henry David Thoreau*

## *Affirmation Do's and Don't's*

As we've seen from the chapters above, there are many ways to make affirmations work really well for *you*, and also many ways that will block their ability to work effectively. Below is a brief summary of the best *do's and don't's* for working with affirmations:

**Positive Do's**

- **Use the present tense.** Stating *'I am healthy'* is more powerful than *'I will be healthy'*, which, logically, means you need to wait for health, rather than realizing the benefits of good health today.

- **Be authentic and believable.** Prevent your subconscious from rejecting your statements by only making true affirmations. Saying *'I am happy'* may not feel as believable as saying *'I choose to be happy today and am open to experiences that make me feel good.'*

- **Be positive.** Statements should only be made using positive language. State *'I am getting healthier every day'* as opposed to *'I will not be ill'*, which focuses your mind on the illness, not the wellness.

- **Block and replace negative thoughts.** Some negative thinking is natural, but don't let it rule your life. Identify your self-destructive thought patterns, and create positive affirmations to replace them.

- **Repeat often.** Make your positive affirmations at least once a day, and repeat them five to ten times on each occasion.

- **Be consistent.** Create a routine that allows you to practice your affirmations daily. Use visual prompts to help build your new affirmation habits.

- **Take action.** Nothing changes unless you are proactive, and take the necessary steps to move toward your desired outcome.

- **Be open.** Notice new opportunities as they present themselves, and willingly receive them into your life.

- **Be thankful.** Take notice of the positive changes that occur in your life, and give thanks for them every day.

- **Expect good things.**

## Problem Don't's

- **Don't expect miracles.** Affirmations take time and effort to get right and to take effect. Be patient, be consistent in your actions, and focus on using effective techniques.

- **Don't try too many at once.** If you tackle too many at the same time, you'll overwhelm your mind, weakening the opportunity for them to take effect.

- **Don't be unrealistic.** Stating *'I am slim'*, and expecting to lose 12 lbs in a matter of a few days won't work, whereas stating *'I am getting closer to my ideal weight every day, and am proud of my achievements',* is more supportive and realistic for your mind to support.

- **Don't give up too soon.** Understand that affirmation habits take time to build, and need your commitment.

- **Don't stop at one thing.** As positive change occurs in one area of your life, move onto another area that you would also like to influence for the better.

- **Don't lose focus.** It's easy to become distracted by daily life, and then forget to practice your affirmations. Find ways to keep your attention attuned to your affirmations, so you can reap the rewards they are capable of delivering.

Although the use of positive affirmations can be tricky to get right, there are steps that can be simple to implement and easy to follow. Focus on doing the right things, avoid the wrong ones, and you'll receive the right results.

## *Positive Affirmation Examples*

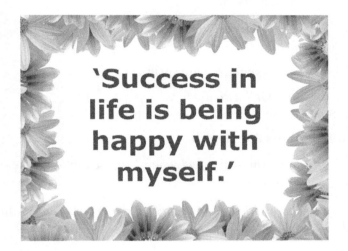

Listed below are some example affirmations. These could be used as you start to craft your own positive, personal belief statements, to inspire, motivate, or encourage you. You could use them as they are, adapt them to suit your own purposes, or simply let them help germinate fresh ideas in your mind.

### Affirmations For Wellbeing

- *'I accept peace, joy, and love into my heart.'*
- *'I am safe and well, and blessed with this life.'*

83

- *'I feel balanced, and have complete inner calm.'*
- *'Good health and wellness is a lifestyle choice for me.'*
- *'With each step I take, I feel better and better, both inside and out.'*
- *'I enjoy a peaceful balance in my mind, body and spirit.'*
- *'I am responsible for my well-being.'*
- *'All is well with my life.'*

## Affirmations For Health

- *'I love the way I feel when I take complete care of myself.'*
- *'Today, I love and respect my body, knowing I am doing my best to keep it healthy.'*
- *'I am ready to be healthy.'*
- *'I only act in the best interests of my body.'*
- *'I choose good health and vitality.'*
- *'I will sleep well tonight, and wake up feeling refreshed and ready to take on the world.'*
- *'My body works hard for me, and I work hard to keep it healthy.'*
- *'I am learning to conquer my anxiety and feel calmer each day.'*

## Affirmations For Healing

- *'I allow healthy, healing energy to enter my body.'*
- *'I give myself permission to heal and feel well again.'*
- *'My strength grows, and my body heals, with every step I take.'*
- *'I acknowledge my fears. I am learning to conquer them, so I can enjoy life to the fullest.'*
- *'I breathe in healing energy, and allow the energy to make every cell in my body healthy.'*
- *'I forgive those who have hurt me in the past, and more forward with a positive attitude.'*
- *'My energy, health and vitality are expanding every day.'*
- *'My body has an amazing capacity for healing.'*
- *'My scars are healed. I am well.'*

## Affirmations For Happiness

- *'I accept positivity into my life.'*
- *'Success in life is being happy with myself.'*
- *'I love myself and allow others to love me, too.'*
- *'I don't need to be perfect, I just enjoy being me.'*
- *'I attract only good things/positive people into my life.'*

- *'This will be a beautiful day, full of happy surprises.'*
- *'As I sleep, I release all negativity, and only have thoughts of happy, joyous times, people, and places.'*
- *'I see opportunities for growth and fulfillment everywhere.'*
- *'I love my smile and want to share it with the world.'*
- *'Today, I choose to be happy.'*

## Affirmations For Success

- *'I expect success.'*
- *'There are no limits to what I can achieve.'*
- *'Each day is a new opportunity to achieve something amazing.'*
- *'My goals are important to me; I won't let fear hold me back.'*
- *'I remove all distractions and obstacles from my path to success.'*
- *'I am proud of myself for my efforts and accomplishments.'*
- *'I give my energy to what I can achieve right now.'*
- *'I trust that my efforts are being rewarded.'*
- *'I am responsible for my own success.'*

## Affirmations For Letting Go

- *'I relinquish anger and resentment.'*
- *'I release all ties that bind me to past issues and hurts.'*
- *'I willingly let go of the old fearful me, and welcome the new confident me.'*
- *'I let go of any resistance to health and healing, and only act in the best interests of my body.'*
- *'I no longer allow negative thoughts or limiting beliefs to prevent me from enjoying life.'*
- *'Fear is only a feeling; it cannot stop me achieving my heart's desire.'*
- *'I willingly accept change, releasing old negative habits.'*
- *'I let go of self-doubt and love my unique qualities'*
- *'Today, I release fear and open my heart to love.'*

## Affirmations For Self Worth

- *'I'm okay just as I am. I'm grateful to be me.'*
- *'I know I am capable of making great things happen in my life.'*
- *'I have the power to choose, to say no, to say yes, to take control.'*
- *'I am ready to express my thoughts and feelings to others, without fear of judgment or criticism.'*

- *'I accept myself unconditionally. I don't need others approval, only to know I've done my best.'*

- *'I focus on the best in everyone and everything, knowing they see the best in me as well.'*

- *'I have the courage to face challenges and find solutions to any problem.'*

- *'My talents and strengths can make a positive difference to the world.'*

- *'I give thanks to myself for what I've achieved today.'*

- *'I choose to be strong and confident.'*

## 5

## Final Thoughts

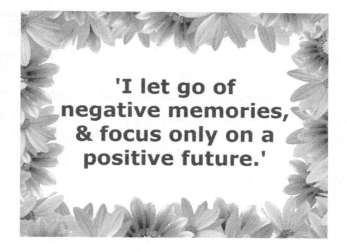

'I let go of negative memories, & focus only on a positive future.'

*"Acceptance makes an incredible fertile soil
for the seeds of change."*
*~ Steve Maraboli*

Using positive affirmations on a daily basis can be an incredibly persuasive method for attracting health, healing, and happiness into each day of your life.

## Remember, as you start each day, it's up to you to decide if it's going to be a positive one.

Everyone has to cope with the onslaught of daily life, and tackle their own personal issues, in areas such as self-esteem, fears, and disappointments. However, by using positive affirmations, you can choose to approach life with a more positive attitude, be open to new opportunities, and expect good things to be attracted effortlessly into your world.

Throughout this book, we've looked at *what, why* and *how* to use positive affirmations to gain personal strength, and to help us feel happy, healthy, and healed.

**We've explored how to:**

- Focus on what you really want.
- Use positive, uplifting, empowering words.
- Re-condition your subconscious, away from toxic thoughts.
- Understand why affirmations can fail.
- Identify the most beneficial affirmations for *you.*
- Correctly use the most effective techniques.
- Create believable statements that feel really good.
- Show gratitude for all positive change.
- Expect good things.

Positive affirmations, when used correctly, can offer a simple, fast and effective method for delivering long lasting change into your life. When you start to believe you are better, both physically and mentally, you will start to receive corresponding physical benefits to your health. When you feel more positive, you enable yourself to cope better with stress, to be more resilient to problems, and to fight off common ailments, thanks to an improved immune system.

Additionally, when you experience positive feelings, either through your engagement of affirmation techniques, or as a result of moving closer to your desired outcome, you will start to see more and more possibilities. As you experience greater levels of emotions, such as contentment, happiness, excitement, joy, and hope, you'll open yourself up to new opportunities, and ways in which you can experience even more of the positive things in life.

**The conscious use of positive affirmations helps to bring about lasting, positive change by creating new affirming beliefs, deep in your subconscious.**

The consistent use of positive affirmations can be a major component in letting go of negative beliefs. They can be used effectively to replace negative self-talk, which, when left unresolved, can have a detrimental effect on both our emotional and physical health, along with our ability to progress in any meaningful manner.

*"Believing in negative thoughts is the single greatest obstruction to success."*
*~ Charles F. Glassman*

There are certain fundamental aspects you need to follow when you embark on a journey of affirmations. **Get these right, and your personal affirmation statements will work amazing well:**

| | |
|---|---|
| **Trust** | Know in your heart that they will work for you |
| **Expectation** | Expect a great outcome |
| **Belief** | Create believable personal statements |
| **Power** | Use your personal powers, and take action |
| **Value** | Be true to yourself and your purpose |
| **Attention** | Give intense focus to what you really want |
| **Gratitude** | Give daily thanks |

Pay attention to these hugely important aspects, as they help fuel the transformations you seek. Understand that each point above brings its own unique benefits, allowing you to continually attract more of what you want into your life.

**Intently focus on what you want to attract**

**The art of positive affirmations needs to be practiced, and honed, and practiced, to become a perfect fit for your own purposes.**

Although affirmations do not necessarily offer a quick fix, they do offer a powerful solution to create positive, lasting change. The creation of well crafted, affirming personal statements, can help recondition our thoughts and beliefs, allowing us to feel good about ourselves in so many different ways.

As they work deeply at the subconscious level to affect change in both your beliefs and attitudes, they can be a driving force for delivering change *exactly* where you want it.

*"A mind that has been stretched
will never return to its
original dimension."*
*~ Albert Einstein*

6

Next Steps

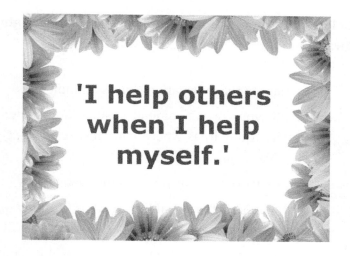

*"All that we are is the result
of what we have thought.
The mind is everything.
What we think we become."*
*~Buddha*

**So,** we know that positive affirmations can help
reprogram your mind to replace negative self-beliefs,

focus your thoughts on positive change, and alter the way you think for good. However...

## What do *you* need to do next, to step into the life you desire?

**Below are some action points to focus on straight away:**

- Commit to the affirmation process completely.
- Create your own personal, positive statements, based on the areas where you most want to see positive change.
- Choose words that inspire and motivate you.
- Add words that are enablers, such as *'learning to, becoming, choose to'*.
- Ensure your statements are believable and authentic.
- Create visual prompts, reminding you to maintain your daily affirmation habits.
- Write your affirmations down, and review them each day.
- Memorize your affirmations, so you can repeat them throughout the day, when the opportunity or need arises.

- Smile, think positive thoughts, and state your affirmations with confidence.
- Practice visualizing your desired outcome.

## *See it, feel it, live it.*

- Begin your day well, by repeating your positive affirmations at the very start.
- End your day with thanks, and recognition of the good things you already have, and are now attracting into your life.
- Remember, you are in control. You can choose to aim your thoughts in whichever direction you desire.

**Review** the various techniques, tools and steps outlined in Chapter 4. Take time to review the many benefits of using affirmations, and consider how you can apply them to serve your own purposes. Focus on taking *effective* steps, and crafting your own empowering personal belief statements. You'll most certainly benefit by feeling more confident, energized, healthier, and in control of the world around you.

**Read** more on the subject of affirmations. If you would like to delve deeper into the incredible benefits of using positive affirmations, then you may also enjoy the following titles by other authors:

*I Can Do It Affirmations: How to Use Affirmations to Change Your Life* – Louise L Hay

*Affirmations Your Passport to Happiness* – Dr. Anne Marie Evers

*Mastering Manifestation: A Practical System For Rapidly Creating Your Dream Reality* – Adam James

*You Can Heal Your Life* – Louise L. Hay

*Creative Visualization: Use the Power of Your Imagination to Create What You Want in Your Life* – Shakti Gawain

*Mind Power Into the 21st Century* – John Kehoe

**Don't over analyze.** Keep things simple and don't fret about the process. Start with a simple affirmation statement; build it up until it feels honest and empowering. Introduce some of the techniques discussed in the chapter on *Effectiveness*, and see which ones have the biggest impact. **If it doesn't feel right, change it. If it feels good, do more of it.**

**Practice, practice, practice.** Take time every day to apply these powerful techniques, and to develop positive personal affirmations that empower you to feel happy, healthy, and healed.

**Take consistent and meaningful steps each day, to work on your personal, empowerment statements and you *will* experience positive, lasting change in your life.**

*"I will always find a way and a way will always find me."*
*~Charles F. Glassman*

## 7

## About The Author

Rachel Robins is the creator behind the feelfabtoday products. She has a passion for exploring and sharing ideas that centre on positivity & self improvement.

Rachel focuses her attention on how to help others feel as good as possible - using realistic feel-good techniques, healthy tips & a hefty dose of positivity. At the heart of the feelfabtoday products are methods on how to feel fabulous, look great, achieve more & live positively. These products are created with the help of a small team of talented people, who add their wisdom, knowledge and skills to the process, and who Rachel would like to thank for their continued efforts and support.

Rachel has worked in various senior management roles, where she's successfully practiced the art of conflict management, leadership, negotiation and change management, plus she's trained many teams and individuals to achieve successful, target driven outcomes. Her range of interpersonal skills, life experience and self-help knowledge means she's able to share practical steps on how to take control of your life, develop a positive self image, and feel good about yourself.

She's put together this FeelFabToday Guide on *Positive Affirmations*, as a source of ideas, inspiration and encouragement, enabling others to craft their own uplifting affirmation statements, and to attract health, healing and happiness into their life. Rachel's also written additional FeelFabToday Guides, designed to explore different areas of self empowerment, confidence building and feeling good about yourself. More information on these Guides can be found at **www.feelfabtoday.com**.

# 8

## And Finally

**We really hope you found
this book helpful.**

*We'd love it if you'd join us at:*
*twitter.com/feelfabtoday*
*www.feelfabtoday.com*
*We also welcome any comments or feedback,*
*so please feel free to get in touch with us:*
*hello@feelfabtoday.com*

Many thanks for reading our book -
we wish you every success in attracting
health, healing, and happiness in to your life...

Made in the USA
Las Vegas, NV
01 May 2024